'Abdu'l-Bahá, Einstein and Ether

By the same author

The Challenge of Bahá'u'lláh
He Cometh With Clouds
Every Eye Shall See
The Metropolis of Satan
Racial Healing in the Bahá'í Faith
Afraid to Speak Against Moses
Muhammad: Defender of Christians

'Abdu'l-Bahá, Einstein and Ether

by

Gary Matthews

Stonehaven Press
3101 Woodbine Ave., Knoxville, TN 37914
1-865-275-5121 (USA)   www.stonehaven-press.com
e-mail: info@stonehaven-press.com

STONEHAVEN PRESS
3101 Woodbine Avenue
Knoxville, Tennessee 37914

phone: 1-865-275-5121 (USA)
web: http://stonehavenpress.com/

ISBN 978-1-893124-04-2

Cover design by Cheri W. Matthews

Contents

The Missing Ether. 7
   A Turning Point for Science. 8
   The First Thread Unravels. 9

The New Physics.. 11
   Sensible vs. Intellectual Realities. 12

Ether's Curious Rise and Fall. 15
   The Rest of the Story. 18
   Expert Testimony. 19

The Question of Precedence. 25

The Collapse of Mechanical Models.. 29
   Overtones of Mysticism. 30
   The Certainty of Uncertainty. 33
   Like a Great Thought. 35

Further Considerations. 37

Scientists Are People. 41
   A War for the Universe.. 41
   Fear of Embarrassment. 42

Einstein on Ether. 45
   Ether and the Theory of Relativity. 49

Bibliography. 61

Acknowledgments.. 63

About the Author. 65

The Missing Ether

The Central Figures of the Bahá'í Faith anticipated in their writings many of the most important discoveries of modern science: atomic energy, transmutation of elements, and space travel, among others. Time and again their predictions have been validated by subsequent research.*

So consistent is this pattern that the Faith's critics, seeking to refute its claim of divine inspiration, have become anxious to find at least one clear-cut scientific error in Bahá'í scriptures.

Perhaps, in some cases, a bit too eager.

* * *

Some now profess to have found such a mistake in 'Abdu'l-Bahá's statements regarding ether – the hypothetical substance once believed, by 19th-century physicists, to pervade all space as a medium for transmitting light, heat and other electromagnetic forces.

It certainly is true that 'Abdu'l-Bahá wrote and spoke repeatedly of ether. There are readers who believe He erred in affirming its existence – an existence (it is said) disproved by Einstein and now universally regarded as a theoretical impossibility.

---

*For details and a variety of examples, see the author's book, *The Challenge of Bahá'u'lláh* (Oxford: George Ronald, Publisher).

This argument is seductively plausible. It is, however, mistaken. A closer look will show that 'Abdu'l-Bahá's statements agree, in intent and substance, with those of the most eminent modern physicists. This turns out to be yet another instance in which Bahá'í prophetic teachings have been validated by the onward march of science.

A Turning Point for Science

Why study ether? Although this topic has fascinated me for many years, I confess to having wondered, now and then, whether that attraction reflects anything more than my own eccentricity. How grateful I was, then, to discover that a large and growing number of Bahá'ís share my own sense of the issue's importance. It now routinely evokes spirited debate in Bahá'í forums for teaching about the Cause. I know devoted believers for whom the ether puzzle has posed a wrenching test of faith. I have met seekers for whom its resolution profoundly influenced their decision whether or not to believe in Bahá'u'lláh, or to join the Bahá'í religion. For others the issue may be purely academic – perhaps as a test case for whichever way we interpret the Bahá'í principle of harmony between science and revelation.

Be that as it may, ether occupies a pivotal position in the history of modern science. Its existence and nature became the primary battlefield, early in the 20th century, for the struggle between the classical physics long associated with Isaac Newton, and the "new physics" identified with Albert Einstein. The latter's victory brought into being the theories of relativity and quantum mechanics. Like the discovery of fire, these have been a mixed blessing: Without them we would have had no atomic bombs, no Hiroshima and Nagasaki, no Chernobyl meltdown, no looming threat of nuclear annihilation. But we also would have had no successful space exploration, no micro-electronics revolution, no computers, no Internet. We would have none of the liberating technologies that led to the tearing-down of the Berlin Wall, the collapse of communism, the end of the Cold War or today's rising tide of globalization – a process Bahá'ís recognize as a necessary prelude to world peace.

Ether was the first domino in the chain of events leading to all of these.

The First Thread Unravels

A crack had appeared in the ether hypothesis as early as 1887, when A.A. Michelson and Edward Morley failed to find relative differences in the speed of light resulting from earth's supposed motion through the ether. This seeming absence of an "ether wind" caused consternation among physicists, who felt obliged to explain it away. They therefore postulated that the earth itself, along with all measuring devices on it, shrank in the direction of its own motion, by an amount just enough to mask the lightspeed differential.

Bizarre as it may sound, we now know that this shrinkage is a reality. (Scientists call it the "Lorentz contraction", after physicist Hendrik Lorentz, who first thought of it.) This did not, however, save ether in anything resembling its classical form. Problems continued to pile up until the publication of Einstein's first relativity paper, a paper modestly titled "On the Electrodynamics of Moving Bodies". This single seminal event swept away the classical ether hypothesis, taking with it the old physics and ultimately the entire old world order.

How strange it would be if the Bahá'í Revelation had nothing to say about events so earth-shaking! The good news is that it has much to say indeed, and that its insights dovetail with the best, most advanced thinking in modern physics.

* * *

Image credits:

Mushroom cloud: U.S. military photo from the bombing of Nagasaki, Japan, on 9 August 1945. Source: Wikimedia Commons.

Ed White, first American spacewalker, 1965: NASA photo. Source: Wikimedia Commons.

Laptop computer: Photo by Gary Matthews.

The New Physics

During the opening decades of the twentieth century, physicists were committed to explaining all phenomena by means of mechanical models. A mechanical model is a precise picture or replica based on human sensory experience. It corresponds in a literally accurate way – not merely a figurative or poetic way – to the thing it represents.

The notion that all reality could be brought under the umbrella of mechanical models was central to "classical" physics (sometimes called Newtonian, after Isaac Newton). Classical physics portrayed the universe as a vast, clockwork machine, all parts of which were in principle completely visualizable.

This plausible interpretation led physicists to regard matter as composed of particles resembling tiny marbles or grains of sand; light, heat, magnetism and similar forces as vibrations, resembling sound waves or ripples in a pond; and time and space as a fixed frame of reference – a limitless arena within which objects and forces interacted but which remained unaffected by their presence.

In such a universe, every event (given enough information) must be completely predictable, for each is predetermined, in all its aspects, by the events that lead up to it.

Most scientists found a mechanistic world view difficult to reconcile with any spiritual or mystical philosophy. Machines are material; and by placing primary emphasis on the material, machine-like aspects of reality, one seems to rule out such abstract concepts as God, the soul, free will and the like. Newton, a devout Christian, would have winced had he realized how powerfully the system of thought associated with his name would promote materialism; yet that is what it did.

Bahá'ís, like other believers in the prophetic revelation, necessarily subscribe to a belief in spiritual realities that do not lend themselves to mechanical interpretation. Our present inquiry, however, concerns none of the metaphysical aspects of such a controversy but only those that are scientifically testable.

Of crucial interest here is 'Abdu'l-Bahá's teaching that even some physical processes (including, among other things, the transmission of light) cannot be faithfully depicted by mechanical models or visualized by the human mind. By so stating, He anticipated some of the twentieth century's most startling discoveries – those that formed the basis of relativity and quantum physics. Let us examine His words more closely.

Sensible vs. Intellectual Realities

All objects of human knowledge, according to 'Abdu'l-Bahá, fall into one of two categories. They are either "sensible realities" or "intellectual realities" (*Some Answered Questions*, p. 83).

Sensible realities, as the name implies, are those we can detect with our physical senses such as sight, hearing and the like. These are the familiar objects of

12

everyday experience – shoes, ships and sealing wax; raindrops and roses; "stuff you can hit with a stick", as someone once explained it. (I suppose 'Abdu'l-Bahá would include under this heading things we can detect only with the aid of physical instruments such as telescopes and infrared goggles, these being extensions of our normal senses.)

An intellectual reality, on the other hand, is one that "has no outward form and no place and is not perceptible to the senses" (*Some Answered Questions*, p. 83). The term "intellectual" in this context does not mean imaginary, nor does it refer exclusively to generalities like "patriotism" or "the square root of pi". As 'Abdu'l-Bahá explains it, the expression includes such intangibles as the human soul and its qualities – realities that exist and produce concrete effects in the world but which are abstract in that they occupy no space and have no specific physical location:

> ". . . if you examine the human body, you will not
> find a special spot or locality for the spirit, for it
> never had a place; it is immaterial. It has a connec-
> tion with the body like that of the sun with this
> mirror. The sun is not within the mirror, but it has
> a connection with the mirror . . . the mind has no
> place, but it is connected with the brain . . . In the
> same way, love has no place, but it is connected with
> the heart; so the Kingdom has no place, but is con-
> nected with man." (*Some Answered Questions*,
> p. 242)

Lacking form, volume and position, an intellectual reality cannot be pictured, nor can it be detected by any

13

physical senses or instruments. "In explaining these intellectual realities," says 'Abdu'l-Bahá, "one is obliged to express them by sensible figures" which have inward rather than outward significance:

> "So the symbol of knowledge is light, and of ignorance, darkness; but reflect, is knowledge sensible light, or ignorance sensible darkness? No, they are merely symbols. These are only intellectual states . . . but when we seek for explanations in the external world, we are obliged to give them sensible form . . . These expressions are metaphors, allegories, mystic explanations in the world of signification." (*Some Answered Questions*, pp. 84-5)

'Abdu'l-Bahá was not content to state this idea simply as a nebulous spiritual precept. Instead, as noted above, He boldly applied it to the physical world in a scientifically testable way. Let us turn now to these scientific implications of His teaching.

Ether's Curious Rise and Fall

The original rationale for ether was simple: Light and similar forces were regarded, during most of the last century, as high-frequency vibrations similar to sound waves. Obviously a vibration must have something in which to vibrate. Physicists reasoned that since light travels through a vacuum, space cannot be truly empty – it must be filled with some invisible, all-penetrating medium that carries the waves.

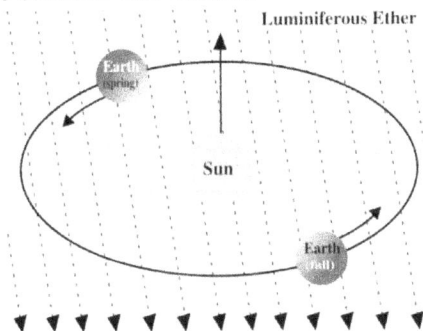

Its odd properties notwithstanding, ether was thus regarded as a physical substance. It was described as having form, volume, density, elasticity and position. It obeyed mechanical laws. Ether not only filled space, but served as an absolute frame of reference marking that space's boundaries (or lack thereof).

It is true that 'Abdu'l-Bahá affirmed the existence of ether:

". . . the nature of ether is unknown, but that it existeth is certain by the effects it produceth, heat, light and electricity being the waves thereof. By these waves the existence of ether is thus proven." (Tablet to August Forel, page 16)

"Thus this light is the vibration of that ethereal matter, and from this vibration we infer the existence of ether." (*Some Answered Questions*, page 190)

"For instance, consider the ethereal element which is penetrating and traveling through all the contingent realities. When there is vibration or movement in the ethereal element, the eye is affected by that vibration and beholds what is known as light." (*Promulgation of Universal Peace*, page 160)

Here, however, is where things become interesting:

In affirming ether, 'Abdu'l-Bahá also redefined it. While saying that "the nature of ether is unknown", He made one extraordinary statement concerning that nature: Ether (He said in a 1905 table-talk) is an "intellectual reality" rather than a physical substance. Such a reality

". . . has no outward form and no place and is not perceptible to the senses . . . Even ethereal matter, the forces of which are said in physics to be heat, light, electricity and magnetism, is an intellectual reality, and is not sensible . . . In explaining these intellectual realities, one is obliged to express them by sensible figures because in exterior existence there is nothing that is not material." (*Some Answered Questions*, pp. 83-84)

In this same passage 'Abdu'l-Bahá likens ether to love, to the human soul or spirit, and to other abstractions. Ether He characterizes as among such "realit[ies] of the intellect" having "no outward form and no place", nor any "exterior existence" because it is "not material".

This explanation is crucial, because the ether of classical physics was anything but an intellectual abstraction. It was conceived as a material substance with definite outward form, a definite place, and definite exterior existence. It had extension and volume (since each cubic foot of space contained one cubic foot of ether) as well as location (for that cube of ether always remained in the same absolute position); and it functioned in a strictly mechanical way. Waves of light moved through the ether exactly as sound waves moved through air, so that one could accurately diagram the process even if the ether itself remained unseen.

'Abdu'l-Bahá's "ether", by contrast, was more like an emotion or a mathematical progression. In redefining ether so radically, He was saying, in effect, that the crude, mechanical ether of contemporary physics did not exist.

Later that same year (1905), the as-yet-unknown Albert Einstein published his historic "special theory" of relativity. He modeled light not as a wave or vibration, but as a stream of particles able to traverse space with no intervening carrier. Space and time he redefined not as a fixed frame of reference, but as mathematical "relativities" among existing objects. In such a model, there is no place for a material ether, which was soon abandoned by most physicists.

The Rest of the Story

Fortunately, this was not the end of the story – merely its beginning:

In his later "general theory" of relativity (1915), Einstein further revolutionized the concepts of space and time. These he merged into a four-dimensional "fabric" or "continuum" with geometrical properties: It could curve, bend, fold, warp, tear, undulate and otherwise undergo astounding contortions. Space remained a mathematical abstraction, but now it came to be viewed also as objectively real. No longer was it a vacuous nothingness, but a "somethingness".

Relativity describes the large-scale universe of stars and galaxies. It was followed in 1927 by quantum mechanics, which describes the small-scale universe of atoms, electrons and quarks. Whereas the space of relativity is a mathematical fabric, that of quantum mechanics is a mathematical "ocean" with a "foamy structure". Its never-ending turbulence manifests itself as the fizz and bubble of ghostly "virtual particles", which pop up out of nowhere, interact briefly, then subside back into the void from which they came. (Except that, as in relativity, such a space really is no longer a void: It is an abstract yet objective reality.)

As the concept of space evolved, so did that of light. Einstein, it turns out, was mistaken in regarding light purely as a particle stream. Niels Bohr in 1927 demonstrated its dual nature: In some unpicturable yet mathematically coherent way, light is both a wave and a particle stream. In its wave aspect, light – like any other vibratory phenomenon – thus retains the need for a medium in which to vibrate.

By this point, however, space itself, as understood by physicists, had grown into the job: It had taken on all necessary properties for such a task. Space itself – or rather, the space-time continuum – is now regarded as the "fabric" or "ocean" through which light waves, gravity waves, and other electro-magnetic forces propagate. Though it has no outward form, no place, no exterior existence, and no material form, it remains an "intellectual reality" in the precise sense described by 'Abdu'l-Bahá.

'Abdu'l-Bahá's ether, in other words, is not a physical substance filling space. It *is* space. Though the name "ether" today is rarely used, this is sheer semantics: The properties of what today's physicists call the "vacuum state" correspond precisely to those He associates with ether.

Expert Testimony

'Abdu'l-Bahá's terminology, though perhaps unorthodox, places Him in stellar company.

Among that company is MIT particle physicist and superstring pioneer Frank Wilczek, who shares a 2004 Nobel Prize for quark research he began during his earlier tenure at Princeton's Institute for Advanced Study.

19

Wilczek made waves worldwide with an essay called "The Persistence of Ether" (*Physics Today*, January 1999). "Quite undeservedly," he writes,

> "the ether has acquired a bad name. There is a myth, repeated in many popular presentations and textbooks, that Albert Einstein swept it into the dustbin of history. The real story is more complicated and interesting. I argue here that the truth is more nearly the opposite: Einstein first purified, and then enthroned, the ether concept. As the 20th century has progressed, its role in fundamental physics has only expanded. At present, renamed and thinly disguised, it dominates the accepted laws of physics. . . .
> "Thus in 1917, following Einstein's revelations, . . . spacetime itself had become a dynamical medium—an ether, if there ever was one. . . . [Later] Paul Dirac showed that photons—Einstein's particles of light—emerged as a logical consequence of applying the laws of quantum mechanics to [James] Maxwell's electromagnetic ether." (For a full-text scanned copy of this paper see *http://ctpweb.lns. mit.edu/physics_today/phystoday/ Ether.pdf*)

In a *New Scientist* article titled "Liquid Space" (November 2001), physicist Paul Davies chronicles this same "surprising revival" through which a retooled "quantum ether" is "creeping back into modern thought." He shows how it is changing the way physicists now look at everything from moving mirrors to black holes to the expansion of the universe itself.

Wilczek and Davies are far from alone. Martin Gardner notes in *Relativity for the Million* that many more prominent physicists have, over the years, proposed restoring the name "ether", though not in the old sense of an immutable frame of reference (Gardner, *Relativity for the Million*, pp. 34-5). A few examples:

✦ Einstein himself, in an address delivered 5 May 1920 at the University of Leiden, says space "is endowed with physical qualities; in this sense, therefore, there exists an ether. According to the general theory of relativity space without ether is unthinkable; for in such space there not only would be no propagation of light, but also no possibility of existence for standards of space and time . . . But this ether may not be thought of as . . . consisting of parts which may be tracked through time. The idea of motion may not be applied to it." (Einstein, *Sidelights on Relativity*, Dover edition, 1983, p. 23. The full text of this address is available for downloading from many sites on the World Wide Web.)

✦ Hendrik Lorentz, the physicist Einstein most admired, reformulated Einstein's relativity equations into his "Lorentz Ether Theory" (LET). Though the two theories are mathematically equivalent and produce identical predictions, LET makes explicit the fact that ether and spacetime likewise have merged into one reality.

21

✦ Nobel laureate Leon Lederman, director-emeritus of Fermilab, observes that "like Pauline's, aether's perils come and go, and today we believe that some new version of aether" is needed to make sense out of current knowledge. "The new aether", he adds, "is then a reference frame for energy, in this case potential energy." (Lederman, *The God Particle*, 101, 375)

✦ Sir Arthur Eddington, who understood relativity theory as well as anyone*, routinely used the traditional term "ether" exactly as 'Abdu'l-Bahá did: He transferred it, that is, to the abstract notion of spacetime invoked by today's authorities. Thus Eddington defines light as "aetherial vibrations of varying wave-lengths" and pictures himself "hanging from a round planet head outward into space, and with a wind of aether blowing at no one knows how many miles a second through every interstice of my body". (Eddington, *Quantum Questions*, pages 189, 208)

---

*Eddington is best known for his eclipse measurements that first verified one of Einstein's special-relativity predictions – that gravity would bend starlight. It is said that Eddington, upon being told he was one of only three people who truly understood Einstein's theory, paused, then said, "I am trying to think who the third person is."

✦ Sir James Jeans writes in a similar vein: "We can now see how the ether, in which all the events of the universe take place, could reduce to a mathematical abstraction and become as abstract and as mathematical as parallels of latitude and meridians of longitude." (Jeans, *Quantum Questions*, page 142)

✦ "Although the classical concept of the ether is now considered obsolete," explains L. Pearce Williams of Cornell University, "the concept of space in modern physics retains certain affinities with an ether: space is not conceived as something totally vacuous but as the seat of various energetic processes." (Williams, "Ether", in *The Encyclopedia Americana*, 1989, vol. X, page 609)

✦ Physicist Charles Misner is still more explicit: "There is a billion dollar industry – the TV industry – which does nothing except produce in empty space potentialities for electrons, were they to be inserted there, to perform some motion. A vacuum so rich in marketable potentialities cannot properly be called a void; it is really an ether." (quoted in Yourgrau and Breck, *Cosmology, History, and Theology*, page 95; and Timothy Ferris, *Coming of Age in the Milky Way*, page 352)

* * *

Image credits:

The Question of Precedence

Since 'Abdu'l-Bahá and Einstein (both of whom agreed in rejecting a physical ether) made their statements on light during the same general period, one may fairly ask whether the Bahá'í leader was simply reacting to news of Einstein's discovery. The answer, so far as I can discover, must be a cautious "no."

Einstein's first relativity paper ("On the Electrodynamics of Moving Bodies") was published in the German *Annals of Physics* in September 1905. 'Abdu'l-Bahá's statement about the non-material nature of ether is found in the book *Some Answered Questions*. The latter comprises 84 talks, covering 1904 through early 1906 and spanning 350 pages in the book's 1964 edition. Individual talks are undated and their chronological order sometimes unclear (since the compiler regrouped them by subject matter). The one in question, however, contains internal evidence that places it toward the beginning or middle of the sequence. This strongly suggests that 'Abdu'l-Baha's explanation predates Einstein's.

In this talk, 'Abdu'l-Bahá discusses the role of symbolism in religious discourse, calling it "a subject that is essential for the comprehension of the questions that we have mentioned, and of others of which we are about to speak". (*Some Answered Questions*, p. 83) A large proportion of the talks throughout the rest of the book seem to take for granted an understanding of the introductory material 'Abdu'l-Bahá presents here. It therefore appears that this talk came early in the series and that the compiler's decision to place it near the front of the book fairly approximates its relative position.

Exact timing aside, Einstein during this period was not a professional scientist but a "technical expert, third class" for the Swiss patent office in Bern. A low-level bureaucrat who knew no scientists, he himself was entirely unknown both to the scientific community and the public. Although he rose to prominence quickly, as such things go, he did not do so overnight. Max Born, one of Europe's top physicists, first learned of Einstein's theory at a physics conference in 1907, a year after the last of the talks in *Some Answered Questions* was delivered. Except for a certain Professor Loria, who brought up his name, neither Born nor any of the other scientists at the conference had even heard of Einstein. "As far as the outside world was concerned," writes his biographer, "he remained totally unknown until 1912, when some aspects of relativity became headline news in Austria. . . ." (Clark, *Einstein*, p. 141)

It is therefore difficult to see how 'Abdu'l-Bahá, isolated from the world in His Turkish prison, entirely lacking in formal education or access to Western media, could have scooped the European physicists to whom the as-yet-unknown Einstein addressed his arguments.

Still, suppose we concede for argument's sake that 'Abdu'l-Bahá might somehow have learned of Einstein and correctly evaluated his discoveries. Even after we grant this quite implausible assumption, we are left with a fact of far greater importance:

While 'Abdu'l-Bahá supported Einstein's conclusion in one respect, He challenged it in another. Both men agreed in denying the existence of a mechanical ether, but Einstein went beyond this by denying that light requires a medium of any kind. 'Abdu'l-Bahá, on the contrary, indicated that light does require a medium, even though that medium has only a conceptual, non-localized form of existence. As the previous chapter shows, a full decade had to pass before this issue could be settled. When this finally occurred, it was Einstein himself who settled it in 'Abdul-Baha's favor.

The Collapse of Mechanical Models

The disappearance of classical ether shook the mechanistic world view but did not, at the outset, destroy it. Scientists continued for some time to believe that everything real is objective, localized and consistent with mechanical models – even those things forever beyond detection by sensory means. They placed in this category the fundamental building blocks of nature itself – namely, subatomic particles.

It was well understood, since early in the 20th century, that things are composed of atoms which in turn are composed of smaller components called protons, neutrons and electrons. The presence of these particles could be deduced from their indirect effects but they could not be sensed or seen, even with the strongest microscope. They simply were too small – so small that any amount of light, even a single photon, would knock them helter-skelter and fail to register them correctly. For all anyone knew, these particles could in turn be further subdivided. (This turns out to be true, at least for protons and neutrons, which are composed of still smaller units called quarks.)

Yet however deeply buried they might be, and whether one pictured them as miniature billiard balls, whirling sparks, or whatnot, the assumption remained that *some* literal image should apply. This meant it should be possible – at least in principle – to build a large-scale replica correctly mimicking the behavior of the atom and all its parts. Classical physics saw nothing wrong with such mechanical yet non-sensible entities.

However, if one accepted at face value 'Abdu'l-Bahá's distinction between "sensible" and "intellectual" realities, a doubt arose. It seemed to rule out not only a mechanical ether but mechanical atoms as well. He had already stated that whatever could not be sensed has "no outward existence", "no outward form and no place". Nor was He timid about applying this principle to the fundamental realities of the physical world. Immediately after His statement redefining ether as a conceptual abstraction, He added: "In the same way, nature, also, in its essence is an intellectual reality and is not sensible" (*Some Answered Questions*, p. 84).

If we could but peer beneath the facade of sense perception (He seemed to be saying), we would find that even the physical world is built upon a foundation that is abstract, unpicturable and non-localized.

Overtones of Mysticism

Though they did not know it then (circa 1905), physicists were about to crack that facade. During the next few years they worked feverishly to make sense of new findings that were pouring in about atomic phenomena. Their objective was to find a workable mechanical model of the atom.

Something, however, was wrong. The more one focused the picture, the fuzzier it became. The mechanical interpretation became increasingly strained and

30

convoluted until scientists, in desperation, were forced to abandon it for theories with strange overtones of mysticism.

First came the revelation (from Einstein's special theory of relativity in 1905) that matter is really congealed energy. Energy is defined in physics as "the capacity to do work"; beyond this, it seems meaningless to ask what energy "really" is. Yet it feels odd to heft a stone and say, "I'm holding a lump of hardened 'capacity to do work'". What could this mean?

A second shock came with the announcement by Niels Bohr, in 1913, that subatomic particles teleport – they move, that is, by vanishing in one spot and popping up in another, without having crossed the intervening space.

The distances involved are short: Longer trips are accomplished by a discontinuous series of short bursts or hops. But without these "quantum leaps" our sun (for example) would freeze and all the stars would wink out. Why? Because stars (including our sun) are powered by nuclear fusion, and fusion occurs when one proton slams into another. Every proton is surrounded by a seamless electrical force-field called the Coulomb barrier. If protons simply moved in continuous lines, they would bounce off the barrier without ever coming into direct contact. In flashing instantly from point to point, however, a fortunate proton sometimes pops through another's shield without having touched it. These lucky hits (called "quantum tunneling" or "quantum teleportation") occur just often enough to create and maintain fusion, keeping stars ablaze.

On the subatomic scale, then, motion is not a flowing blend but a pattern of jumps, more like a Charlie Chaplin movie than a Baryshnikov ballet. Just as the still frames of a movie create the illusion of continuity, so do the quantum leaps of moving matter.

Physicists gulped, but – having no choice – swallowed this odd picture.

A third jolt came as they realized that the exact distance, direction and timing of each jump seemed, within limits, to be quite random. The absolute predestination implied by Newtonian mechanism was a myth, since the past history of a particle did not completely determine its next move. Einstein, already nervous about where particle physics seemed headed, lost his patience over this one. "I find the idea quite intolerable", he wrote, "that an electron exposed to radiation should choose *of its own free will*, not only its moment to jump off, but also its direction." (Einstein, quoted in Born, *The Born-Einstein Letters*, p. 82; and Ferris, *Coming of Age,* p. 290; Einstein's italics) He argued that "hidden variables", unknown and undetectable, must be in control.

However, physicist John S. Bell later found a theorem proving that such variables, if they existed, would have to be capable of affecting events instantaneously throughout the universe. Since a basic premise of Einstein's theory is that no physical signal can travel faster than light, any hidden variables would "border on what we now call psychic phenomena" (Wolf, *Taking the Quantum Leap*, p. 201). This seemed even stranger and less mechanical than the picture Einstein rejected.

Stranger still: Just as light waves sometimes behave like particles, so too do matter particles sometimes act like waves. For example, a single electron will spread like a wave, passing through two slits of a screen at the same time and producing an interference pattern – yet any and all efforts to observe it detect only a pinpoint. Its behaviour is described by the "Schrödinger pulse", a mathematical wave function with no recognizable form in physical space. It does not resemble a water wave, a sound wave, or any other familiar analogy.

The Certainty of Uncertainty

The decisive break with classical mechanics came in 1927 when Werner Heisenberg unveiled his famous uncertainty principle. This concerns the position and velocity of a subatomic particle. (Velocity is a combination of speed and direction; it is the mathematical description of a particle's motion.)

On a superficial level, the uncertainty principle means we cannot precisely measure both the position and the velocity of a particle at the same time. Any method we use to evaluate one will perturb the other, so that we can never know both with complete accuracy.

Unfortunately, a great many popular works on science give the misleading impression that there is nothing more to the uncertainty principle than that: Nature (they imply) is simply hiding from our clumsy methods. If this were so, the principle would never have been the shattering revelation it was.

What Heisenberg found is not simply that we cannot *know* the precise position and velocity of a particle at the same time. He found that it cannot *have* them both at the same time. The special "matrix" mathematics governing subatomic behaviour precludes the very existence of such simultaneous variables. The more there is to know about one, the less there is to know about the other – regardless of what we actually know. The more accurately we measure a particle's position, the more fuzzy its velocity becomes; and the more accurately we measure its velocity, the more fuzzy its position becomes. This fuzziness is not only in our minds; it is a property of the particle itself.

What of an unobserved particle? According to the standard interpretation of quantum mechanics, such a particle has an infinite number of different positions and velocities (a blur of overlapping histories, so to speak), each more or less probable, but none completely real. The particle is nothing more than a ghostly potentiality, a swirl of mutually exclusive possibilities each vying for the right to exist. By choosing to observe either its position or its velocity (for we cannot do both), we make the particle more real in that respect, but at the cost of making it less real in the other.

The thundering implications of the uncertainty principle have barely begun to penetrate modern thought. Even many professional philosophers seem strangely deaf to its rumble. Physics, says John A. Wheeler, has "destroyed the concept of the world as 'sitting out there'. The universe will never afterwards be the same." (John A. Wheeler, quoted in Wolf, *Taking the Quantum Leap*, p. 152) Quantum mechanics portrays the world not as a collection of concrete objects, nor even as tiny bits of "stuff" swarming through mostly empty space, but as a statistical composite of shifting probabilities. Any large-scale object is a vast collection of such quasi-abstract entities – entities which, by augmenting one another, invest the object with a semblance of position, motion and recognizable form. Each in itself, however, is entirely unpicturable, with no distinct location in space and time.

Modern physics thus confirms what 'Abdu'l-Bahá taught long before: The natural universe below the reach of sense perception is, in its essence, utterly incompatible with mechanical models. We can describe it not by any literal image but only by symbols and metaphors. "When it comes to atoms," writes Niels Bohr, "language can be used only as in poetry." (Bohr, quoted in Ferris, *Coming of Age*, p. 384)

Like a Great Thought

The subjective, non-local nature of the material universe is no mere philosophical teaser; it can be – and has been – tested by laboratory experiment. John Clauser, a physicist with the University of California at Berkeley, is one who has done so, using insights derived from the Bell theorem mentioned above. Summarizing his results, he writes:

> "Physicists have consistently attempted to model microscopic phenomena in terms of objective entities, preferably with some definable structure . . . . We have found that it is not possible to do so in a

natural way, consistent with locality, without an observable change in the experimental predictions." (Clauser, quoted in *Taking the Quantum Leap*, p. 206)

It is fitting that physics – the most concrete of the so-called "hard sciences" – was the first to confirm the metaphorical nature of physical reality affirmed by 'Abdu'l-Bahá. Since the dawn of quantum mechanics in the 1920s, virtually every major physics breakthrough has in some way reinforced this outlook. The result has been, in the words of Sir James Jeans, "a wide measure of agreement which, on the physical side of science, approaches almost to unanimity that the stream of knowledge is heading towards a nonmechanical reality; the universe begins to look more like a great thought than like a great machine." (Jeans, *Quantum Questions*, p. 144)

* * *

Image credits:
Werner Heisenberg, 1933: From German Federal Archives. Licensed under Creative Commons Attribution-Share Alike Germany 3.0. Source: Wikimedia Commons.

Further Considerations

Most of the above information is found, in somewhat greater detail, in my 1993 book *The Challenge of Bahá'u'lláh* (reprinted in 1999 by George Ronald, Publisher, of Oxford). So far as I know, this book contained the first *published* effort to correlate 'Abdu'l-Bahá's statements about ether with the findings of modern physics.

I soon learned, however, that other Bahá'ís already had discovered this same information. While *Challenge* was in its final stages of editing and production, I received the following letter from the World Center Research Department, in reply to an inquiry I had written on 24 April 1992:

> "The Australian Association of Bahá'í Studies Conferences has included discussion of this question at meetings held in that country over the past several years. Although the transcripts of the oral presentations made at these meeting are not available at the Bahá'í World Center, it appears from notes and unpublished papers which are available here that the approach used in those presentations has been to distinguish between two quite different concepts of the ether: One is the traditional and now discredited view that it is a medium having properties measurable by physical experimentation; the other is the definition found acceptable to scientists such as

Einstein in his later years and consistent with the properties attributed to empty space by the electromagnetic and gravitational fields. The argument presented in this approach is that the latter definition of the term ether is in conformity with the usage adopted by 'Abdu'l-Bahá where He states that '. . . ethereal matter, the forces of which are said in physics to be heat, light, electricity and magnetism, is an intellectual reality, and is not sensible. . . .' and defines such an intellectual reality as one which '. . . has no outward form and no place and is not perceptible to the senses. . . .'" (17 July 1992)

When the book *Messages from the Universal House of Justice: 1963-1986* appeared in 1996, I learned to my delight that the House of Justice had confirmed this approach a decade earlier. In replying to an individual, that body wrote:

"With reference to your question about the 'ether', the various definitions of this word as given in the *Oxford English Dictionary* all refer to a physical reality, for instance, 'an element', 'a substance', 'a medium', all of which imply a physical and objective reality and, as you say, this was the concept posited by 19th-century scientists to explain the propagation of light waves. It would have been understood in this sense by the audiences whom 'Abdu'l-Bahá was addressing. However, in Chapter XVI of *Some Answered Questions*, 'Abdu'l-Bahá devotes a whole chapter to explaining the difference between things which are 'perceptible to the senses' which He calls 'objective or sensible', and realities of the 'intellect' which have 'no outward form and no place', and are 'not perceptible to the senses'. He gives examples of both 'kinds' of 'human knowledge'. The first kind is obvious and does not need elaboration. To illustrate the second kind the examples He gives are: love, grief, happiness, the power of the intellect, the human spirit and 'ethereal matter'. (In the original Persian the word 'ethereal' is the same as 'etheric'.) He states clearly that 'Even ethereal matter, the forces of which are said in physics to be heat, light, electricity and magnetism, is an intellectual reality, and is not sensible.' In other words, the 'ether' is a concept arrived at intellectually to explain certain phenomena. In due course, when scientists failed to confirm the physical existence of the 'ether' by delicate experiments, they constructed other intellectual concepts to explain the same phenomena." (3 June 1982; *Messages*, pp. 546-547)

All these observations boil down to a single point: 'Abdu'l-Bahá explicitly redefined ether in a manner contrary to the physics of His own day, but completely consonant with that of ours. Is it not significant that different Bahá'ís, researching the question independently in Australia, Israel and North America, consistently reach this same conclusion? Should this understanding not be similarly obvious to anyone who studies 'Abdu'l-Bahá's pronouncements through the lens of physics history?

If it is not, that may be because we so easily forget the human side of science which this history illustrates. Let us explore this angle a bit further.

Scientists Are People

According to a pervasive stereotype, the so-called "hard sciences" (physics, chemistry, biology, astronomy and others concerned with material reality) are dominated by "laboratory fact", by objective knowledge, by rigorous measurement. We assume that such disciplines produce conclusions of a more or less absolute nature – black-and-white "findings" or "verdicts" no longer open to further discussion.

The reality – as any competent scientist will attest – is that science is a human enterprise involving subjectivity, semantics and value judgments. Real science, including physics, seldom if ever produces "verdicts". It suggests provisional hypotheses – models marked not by finality, but by its opposite. The strength of science is its self-correcting openness to new evidence, through the constant testing and refining of its own most cherished assumptions. This never-ending process is influenced not only by objective data, but by social and personal factors.

A War for the Universe

We see this clearly in the ether controversy. The early decades of the 20th century saw a battle royal between the "new physics" of Einstein, Heisenberg and Bohr, and the "classical physics" long associated with Newton. So wrenching was this struggle that Einstein himself, with regard to quantum mechanics, found himself straddling its fence! During this epoch, ether – defined as a material substance – became a rallying cry for rear-guard physicists striving vainly to turn back the new wind. Born as a technical construct, ether suddenly found itself a pawn in what amounted to a war for the universe.

The new physics prevailed because it was more coherent and predictively powerful than that of Newton. As it arose, many classical ideas, such as "mass" and "motion", were profoundly redefined – old labels being transferred to new mathematical models. The ether concept could have been similarly updated, and probably would have been, had it not been caught instead in an ideological crossfire. By discarding this emotionally charged label, the physics community symbolically voted for Einstein against his by-now-discredited opponents. (Even prestigious scientists have been known to enjoy backing a winner – especially one as gracious and humble as Einstein.)

The ideological crossfire escalated further with the rise and reign of Adolph Hitler in Einstein's native land. During this period, the most strident and vocal opponents of relativity tended to associate themselves with Nazism in an effort to purify traditional "German science" from what they saw as the taint of Einstein's "Jewish science". As a result, ether acquired Nazi connotations from which responsible physicists recoiled.

Fear of Embarrassment

A further factor may have been simple embarrassment. The word "ether" was dropped during that brief interlude when there seemed to be no place, in Einstein's scheme, for a light-bearing medium. Once it became clear that such a vehicle was needed after all, physicists faced a choice: Reinstate the old word, or invent new terminology. But we can all too well imagine the result had they announced that "ether is back" – having just kicked it out. Physicists would have been the butt of jokes by stand-up comics and newspaper editorials: "They can't make up their minds!" The danger of such unfair carping was real: Pundits long have taken glee in poking fun at bespectacled scientists, and the latter naturally resent such stereotyping.

There thus arose an irresistible temptation to smuggle the new-and-improved ether back in through the back door – "renamed and thinly disguised", as Wilczek explains: Call it a "field", a "fabric", an "ocean", a "continuum", a "vacuum state" or whatnot. Anything but ether!

By any other name, however, it does the same job. The authorities quoted above – who confirm the substance of 'Abdu'l-Bahá's views, using terminology substantially identical to His own – are hardly second-stringers. Even to call them top-flight, world-class physicists is to greatly understate their prominence.

Thus 'Abdu'l-Bahá's exposition of ether represents not an error, but a stunning triumph of His prophetic vision.

Einstein on Ether

From 1905 until 1916, Einstein more or less rejects altogether the concept of ether. As explained previously, it seemed superfluous from the standpoint of "special" relativity, the narrow, early version of his theory.

In the wake of his later, greatly expanded theory of "general" relativity, several physicists – notably H.A. Lorentz and Philipp Lenard – challenged him to recognize that "spacetime" is simply a new name for ether – an ether stripped of mechanical properties.

Einstein first embraces this paradigm shift in a letter to Lorentz, dated 17 June 1916:

> "I agree with you that the general theory of relativity is closer to the ether hypothesis than the special theory. This new ether theory, however, would not violate the principle of relativity, because the state of this . . . ether would not be that of rigid body in an independent state of motion, but every state of motion would be a function of position determined by material processes." (Einstein Archives, 16-453)

But his first published statement to this effect comes in 1918:

> "Whereas according to the special theory of relativity a part of space without matter and without electromagnetic field seems to be completely empty,

that is to say not characterized by any physical properties, according to the general theory of relativity even space that is empty in this sense has physical properties. . . . This state of things can be easily understood by speaking about an ether, whose state varies continuously from point to point. One must only be careful not to attribute to this 'ether' the properties of ordinary material bodies (e.g., a well defined velocity at every point)." (*Dialog über Einwände gegen die Relativitätstheorie*, Die Naturwissenschaften, 6 [1918] 697-702)

In this same paper, Einstein proclaims once again that the "ether *in the old sense* does not exist" (emphasis added).

In the "Morgan Manuscript" (1920), he writes:

"Thus, once again 'empty' space appears as endowed with physical properties, i.e., no longer as physically empty, as seemed to be the case according to special relativity. One can thus say that the *ether is resurrected in the general theory of relativity*, though in a more sublimated form." (Einstein Archives 2070; emphasis added)

In 1924:

"[...] we will not be able to do without the ether in theoretical physics, i.e., a continuum which is equipped with physical properties; for the general theory, whose basic points of view physicists surely will always maintain, excludes direct distant action. But every contiguous action theory presumes continuous fields, and therefore also the existence of an 'ether'." (*Über den Äther, Vierteljahresschrift der naturforschenden Geselschaft*, Zurich, 105 ([1924] 85-93)

Again, ten years later:

"Physical space and ether are only different terms for the same thing; fields are physical states of space." (*Das Raum-, Äther- und Feld- Problem der Physik*, in: A. Einstein, Mein Weltbild. Amsterdam: Querido, 1934, pp. 229-248)

And in 1938 (with L. Infeld) he writes:

"We may still use the word ether, but only to express the physical properties of space. The word ether has changed its meaning many times in the development of science. At the moment, it no longer stands for a medium built up of particles. Its story, by no means finished, is continued by the relativity theory." (*Die Physik als Abenteur der Erkenntnis, Leiden*, A W. Sijthofs Witgeversmaatschappij N. V., 1949, pp. 99-100)

Having accepted this revised ether, Einstein – as these citations show – expounded it over a span of decades. To the best of our knowledge, he retained this opinion until his death in 1955.

(Many of the quotations cited above first appeared in English translation in Ludwik Kostro's book, *Einstein and the Ether,* published in 2000. Kostro is a professor of physics at the University of Gdansk in Poland.)

The talk quoted earlier in this book, given at the University of Leiden in 1920, is among Einstein's earlier statements along these lines. It is also perhaps the most comprehensive. Renouncing mathematics and technical jargon, Einstein instead provides an illuminating history of ether's evolution as a scientific hypothesis. He refers repeatedly to the human side of science – to the various ways in which (for example) emotional discomfort, playfulness, aesthetic sensibilities, and other personality traits may influence a scientist's outlook.

Given the talk's importance, it seems fitting to close this section by reprinting its full text:

Ether and the Theory of Relativity
by Albert Einstein

(5 May 1920, University of Leiden)

How does it come about that alongside of the idea of ponderable matter, which is derived by abstraction from everyday life, the physicists set the idea of the existence of another kind of matter, the ether? The explanation is probably to be sought in those phenomena which have given rise to the theory of action at a distance, and in the properties of light which have led to the undulatory theory. Let us devote a little while to the consideration of these two subjects.

Outside of physics we know nothing of action at a distance. When we try to connect cause and effect in the experiences which natural objects afford us, it seems at first as if there were no other mutual actions than those of immediate contact, e.g. the communication of motion by impact, push and pull, heating or inducing combustion by means of a flame, etc. It is true that even in everyday experience weight, which is in a sense action at a distance, plays a very important part. But since in daily experience the weight of bodies meets us as something constant, something not linked to any cause which is variable in time or place, we do not in everyday life speculate as to the cause of gravity, and therefore do not become conscious of its character as action at a distance. It was Newton's theory of gravitation that first assigned a cause for gravity by interpreting it as action at a distance, proceeding from masses. Newton's theory is probably the greatest stride ever made in the effort towards the causal nexus of natural phenomena. And yet this theory evoked a lively sense of discomfort among Newton's contemporaries, because it seemed to be in conflict with the principle springing from the rest of experience, that there can be reciprocal action only through contact, and not through immediate action at a distance.

It is only with reluctance that man's desire for knowledge endures a dualism of this kind. How was unity to be preserved in his comprehension of the forces of nature? Either by trying to look upon contact forces as being themselves distant forces which admittedly are observable only at a very small distance and this was the road which Newton's followers, who were entirely under the spell of his doctrine, mostly preferred to take; or by assuming that the Newtonian action at a distance is only apparently immediate action at a distance, but in truth is conveyed by a medium permeating space, whether by movements or by elastic deformation of this medium. Thus the endeavour toward a unified view of the nature of forces leads to the hypothesis of an ether. This hypothesis, to be sure, did not at first bring with it any advance in the theory of gravitation or in physics generally, so that it became customary to treat Newton's law of force as an axiom not further reducible. But the ether hypothesis was bound always to play some part in physical science, even if at first only a latent part.

When in the first half of the nineteenth century the far-reaching similarity was revealed which subsists between the properties of light and those of elastic waves in ponderable bodies, the ether hypothesis found fresh support. It appeared beyond question that light must be interpreted as a vibratory process in an elastic, inert medium filling up universal space. It also seemed to be a necessary consequence of the fact that light is capable of polarisation that this medium, the ether, must be of the nature of a solid body, because transverse waves are not possible in a fluid, but only in a solid. Thus the physicists were bound to arrive at the theory of the "quasi-rigid" luminiferous ether, the parts of which can carry out no move-ments relatively to one another except the small movements of deformation which correspond to light-waves.

This theory - also called the theory of the stationary luminiferous ether - moreover found a strong support in an experiment which is also of fundamental importance in the special theory of relativity, the experiment of Fizeau, from which one was obliged to infer that the luminiferous ether does not take part in the movements of bodies. The phenomenon of aberration also favoured the theory of the quasi-rigid ether.

The development of the theory of electricity along the path opened up by Maxwell and Lorentz gave the development of our ideas concerning the ether quite a peculiar and unexpected turn. For Maxwell himself the ether indeed still had properties which were purely mechanical, although of a much more complicated kind than the mechanical properties of tangible solid bodies. But neither Maxwell nor his followers succeeded in elaborating a mechanical model for the ether which might furnish a satisfactory mechanical interpretation of Maxwell's laws of the electro-magnetic field. The laws were clear and simple, the mechanical interpretations clumsy and contradic-tory. Almost imperceptibly the theoretical physicists adapted themselves to a situation which, from the standpoint of their mechanical programme, was very depressing. They were particularly influenced by the electro-dynamical investigations of Heinrich Hertz. For whereas they previously had required of a conclusive theory that it should content itself with the funda-mental concepts which belong exclusively to mechanics (e.g. densities, velocities, deformations, stresses) they gradually accustomed themselves to admitting electric and magnetic force as fundamental concepts side by side with those of mechanics, without requiring a mechanical interpretation for them. Thus the purely mechanical view of nature was gradually abandoned. But this change led to a fundamental dualism which in the long-run was insupportable. A way of escape was now sought in the reverse direction, by reducing the principles of mechanics to those of electricity, and this especially as confidence in the strict validity of the equations of Newton's mechanics was shaken by the experiments with b-rays and rapid cathode rays.

This dualism still confronts us in unextenuated form in the theory of Hertz, where matter appears not only as the bearer of velocities, kinetic energy, and mechanical pressures, but also as the bearer of electromagnetic fields. Since such fields also occur in vacuo - i.e. in free ether-the ether also appears as bearer of electromagnetic fields. The ether appears indistinguishable in its functions from ordinary matter. Within matter it takes part in the motion of matter and in empty space it has everywhere a velocity; so that the ether has a definitely assigned velocity throughout the whole of space. There is no fundamental difference between Hertz's ether and ponderable matter (which in part subsists in the ether).

The Hertz theory suffered not only from the defect of ascribing to matter and ether, on the one hand mechanical states, and on the other hand electrical states, which do not stand in any conceivable relation to each other; it was also at variance with the result of Fizeau's important experiment on the velocity of the propagation of light in moving fluids, and with other established experimental results.

Such was the state of things when H A Lorentz entered upon the scene. He brought theory into harmony with experience by means of a wonderful simplification of theoretical principles. He achieved this, the most important advance in the theory of electricity since Maxwell, by taking from ether its mechanical, and from matter its electromagnetic qualities. As in empty space, so too in the interior of material bodies, the ether, and not matter viewed atomistically, was exclusively the seat of electromagnetic fields. According to Lorentz the elementary particles of matter alone are capable of carrying out movements; their electromagnetic activity is entirely confined to the carrying of electric charges. Thus Lorentz succeeded in reducing all electromagnetic happenings to Maxwell's equations for free space.

As to the mechanical nature of the Lorentzian ether, it may be said of it, in a somewhat playful spirit, that immobility is the only mechanical property of which it has not been deprived by H A Lorentz. It may be added that the whole change in the conception of the ether which the special theory of relativity brought about, consisted in taking away from the ether its last mechanical quality, namely, its immobility. How this is to be understood will forthwith be expounded.

The space-time theory and the kinematics of the special theory of relativity were modelled on the Maxwell-Lorentz theory of the electromagnetic field. This theory therefore satisfies the conditions of the special theory of relativity, but when viewed from the latter it acquires a novel aspect. For if K be a system of coordinates relatively to which the Lorentzian ether is at rest, the Maxwell-Lorentz equations are valid primarily with reference to K. But by the special theory of relativity the same equations without any change of meaning also hold in relation to any new system of co-ordinates K' which is moving in uniform translation relatively to K. Now comes the anxious question: Why must I in the theory distinguish the K system above all K' systems, which are physically equivalent to it in all respects, by assuming that the ether is at rest relatively to the K system? For the theoretician such an asymmetry in the theoretical structure, with no corresponding asymmetry in the system of experience, is intolerable. If we assume the ether to be at rest relatively to K, but in motion relatively to K', the physical equivalence of K and K' seems to me from the logical standpoint, not indeed down-right incorrect, but nevertheless unacceptable.

The next position which it was possible to take up in face of this state of things appeared to be the following. The ether does not exist at all. The electromagnetic fields are not states of a medium, and are not bound down to any bearer, but they are independent realities which are not reducible to anything else, exactly like the atoms of ponderable matter. This conception suggests itself the more readily as, according to Lorentz's theory, electromagnetic radiation, like ponderable matter, brings impulse and energy with it, and as, according to the special theory of relativity, both matter and radiation are but special forms of distributed energy, ponderable mass losing its isolation and appearing as a special form of energy.

More careful reflection teaches us however, that the special theory of relativity does not compel us to deny ether. We may assume the existence of an ether; only we must give up ascribing a definite state of motion to it, i.e. we must by abstraction take from it the last mechanical characteristic which Lorentz had still left it. We shall see later that this point of view, the conceivability of which I shall at once endeavour to make more intelligible by a somewhat halting comparison, is justified by the results of the general theory of relativity.

Think of waves on the surface of water. Here we can describe two entirely different things. Either we may observe how the undulatory surface forming the boundary between water and air alters in the course of time; or else-with the help of small floats, for instance - we can observe how the position of the separate particles of water alters in the course of time. If the existence of such floats for tracking the motion of the particles of a fluid were a fundamental impossibility in physics - if, in fact nothing else whatever were observable than the shape of the space occupied by the water as it varies in time, we should have no ground for the assumption that water consists of movable particles. But all the same we could characterise it as a medium.

We have something like this in the electromagnetic field. For we may picture the field to ourselves as consisting of lines of force. If we wish to interpret these lines of force to ourselves as something material in the ordinary sense, we are tempted to interpret the dynamic processes as motions of these lines of force, such that each separate line of force is tracked through the course of time. It is well known, however, that this way of regarding the electromagnetic field leads to contradictions.

Generalising we must say this:- There may be supposed to be extended physical objects to which the idea of motion cannot be applied. They may not be thought of as consisting of particles which allow themselves to be separately tracked through time. In Minkowski's idiom this is expressed as follows:- Not every extended conformation in the four-dimensional world can be regarded as composed of world-threads. The special theory of relativity forbids us to assume the ether to consist of particles observable through time, but the hypothesis of ether in itself is not in conflict with the special theory of relativity. Only we must be on our guard against ascribing a state of motion to the ether.

Certainly, from the standpoint of the special theory of relativity, the ether hypothesis appears at first to be an empty hypothesis. In the equations of the electromagnetic field there occur, in addition to the densities of the electric charge, only the intensities of the field. The career of electromagnetic processes in vacuo appears to be completely determined by these equations, uninfluenced by other physical quantities. The electromagnetic fields appear as ultimate, irreducible realities, and at first it seems superfluous to postulate a homogeneous, isotropic ether-medium, and to envisage electromagnetic fields as states of this medium.

But on the other hand there is a weighty argument to be adduced in favour of the ether hypothesis. To deny the ether is ultimately to assume that empty space has no physical qualities whatever. The fundamental facts of mechanics do not harmonize with this view. For the mechanical behaviour of a corporeal system hovering freely in empty space depends not only on relative positions (distances) and relative velocities, but also on its state of rotation, which physically may be taken as a characteristic not appertaining to the system in itself. In order to be able to look upon the rotation of the system, at least formally, as something real, Newton objectivises space. Since he classes his absolute space together with real things, for him rotation relative to an absolute space is also something real. Newton might no less well have called his absolute space "Ether"; what is essential is merely that besides observable objects, another thing, which is not perceptible, must be looked upon as real, to enable acceleration or rotation to be looked upon as something real.

It is true that Mach tried to avoid having to accept as real something which is not observable by endeavouring to substitute in mechanics a mean acceleration with reference to the totality of the masses in the universe in place of an acceleration with reference to absolute space. But inertial resistance opposed to relative acceleration of distant masses presupposes action at a distance; and as the modern physicist does not believe that he may accept this action at a distance, he comes back once more, if he follows Mach, to the ether, which has to serve as medium for the effects of inertia. But this conception of the ether to which we are led by Mach's way of thinking differs essentially from the ether as conceived by Newton, by Fresnel, and by Lorentz. Mach's ether not only conditions the behaviour of inert masses, but is also conditioned in its state by them.

Mach's idea finds its full development in the ether of the general theory of relativity. According to this theory the metrical qualities of the continuum of space-time differ in the environment of different points of space-time, and are partly conditioned by the matter existing outside of the territory under consideration. This space-time variability of the reciprocal relations of the standards of space and time, or, perhaps, the recognition of the fact that "empty space" in its physical relation is neither homogeneous nor isotropic, compelling us to describe its state by ten functions (the gravitation potentials gmn), has, I think, finally disposed of the view that space is physically empty. But therewith the conception of the ether has again acquired an intelligible content although this content differs widely from that of the ether of the mechanical undulatory theory of light. The ether of the general theory of relativity is a medium which is itself devoid of all mechanical and kinematical qualities, but helps to determine mechanical (and electromagnetic) events.

What is fundamentally new in the ether of the general theory of relativity as opposed to the ether of Lorentz consists in this, that the state of the former is at every place determined by connections with the matter and the state of the ether in neighbouring places, which are amenable to law in the form of differential equations; whereas the state of the Lorentzian ether in the absence of electromagnetic fields is conditioned by nothing outside itself, and is everywhere the same. The ether of the general theory of relativity is transmuted conceptually into the ether of Lorentz if we substitute constants for the functions of space which describe the former, disregarding the causes which condition its state. Thus we may also say, I think, that the ether of the general theory of relativity is the outcome of the Lorentzian ether, through relativation.

As to the part which the new ether is to play in the physics of the future we are not yet clear. We know that it determines the metrical relations in the space-time continuum, e.g. the configurative possibilities of solid bodies as well as the gravitational fields; but we do not know whether it has an essential share in the structure of the electrical elementary particles constituting matter. Nor do we know whether it is only in the proximity of ponderable masses that its structure differs essentially from that of the Lorentzian ether; whether the geometry of spaces of cosmic extent is approximately Euclidean. But we can assert by reason of the relativistic equations of gravitation that there must be a departure from Euclidean relations, with spaces of cosmic order of magnitude, if there exists a positive mean density, no matter how small, of the matter in the universe.

In this case the universe must of necessity be spatially unbounded and of finite magnitude, its magnitude being determined by the value of that mean density.

If we consider the gravitational field and the electromagnetic field from the standpoint of the ether hypothesis, we find a remarkable difference between the two. There can be no space nor any part of space without gravitational potentials; for these confer upon space its metrical qualities, without which it cannot be imagined at all. The existence of the gravitational field is inseparably bound up with the existence of space. On the other hand a part of space may very well be imagined without an electromagnetic field; thus in contrast with the gravitational field, the electromagnetic field seems to be only secondarily linked to the ether, the formal nature of the electromagnetic field being as yet in no way determined by that of gravitational ether. From the present state of theory it looks as if the electromagnetic field, as opposed to the gravitational field, rests upon an entirely new formal motif, as though nature might just as well have endowed the gravitational ether with fields of quite another type, for example, with fields of a scalar potential, instead of fields of the electromagnetic type.

Since according to our present conceptions the elementary particles of matter are also, in their essence, nothing else than condensations of the electromagnetic field, our present view of the universe presents two realities which are completely separated from each other conceptually, although connected causally, namely, gravitational ether and electromagnetic field, or - as they might also be called - space and matter.

Of course it would be a great advance if we could succeed in comprehending the gravitational field and the electromagnetic field together as one unified conformation. Then for the first time the epoch of theoretical physics founded by Faraday and Maxwell would reach a satisfactory conclusion. The contrast between ether and matter would fade away, and, through the general theory of relativity, the whole of physics would become a complete system of thought, like geometry, kinematics, and the theory of gravitation. An exceedingly ingenious attempt in this direction has been made by the mathematician H Weyl; but I do not believe that his theory will hold its ground in relation to reality. Further, in contemplating the immediate future of theoretical physics we ought not unconditionally to reject the possibility that the facts comprised in the quantum theory may set bounds to the field theory beyond which it cannot pass.

Recapitulating, we may say that according to the general theory of relativity space is endowed with physical qualities; in this sense, therefore, there exists an ether. According to the general theory of relativity space without ether is unthinkable; for in such space there not only would be no propagation of light, but also no possibility of existence for standards of space and time (measuring-rods and clocks), nor therefore any space-time intervals in the physical sense. But this ether may not be thought of as endowed with the quality characteristic of ponderable media, as consisting of parts which may be tracked through time. The idea of motion may not be applied to it.

Bibliography

Insofar as possible, I have tried to quote current editions of Bahá'í sacred texts and to identify those editions precisely in this bibliography. New editions, however, appear frequently. For any particular book, it is always possible that the version I used will differ in page numbering or other minor respects from the one available to a given reader.

One welcome antidote to such confusion is the online Bahá'í Reference Library (*http://reference.bahai.org*). This site provides electronic access to a comprehensive database of Bahá'í authoritative texts in English, Persian, and Arabic. To locate the most current, "standard" source for any quoted passage, simply enter a fragment of its text into the search box. This will call up the complete passage, along with full context and up-to-date page and paragraph numbering.

'ABDU'L-BAHÁ. *Some Answered Questions*. Collected and translated from the Persian by Laura Clifford Barney. Wilmette: Bahá'í Publishing Trust, 1984.

— *The Promulgation of Universal Peace*. Talks delivered by 'Abdu'l-Bahá during His visit to the United States and Canada in 1912. Wilmette: á'í Publishing Trust, 1982.

— "Tablet to Auguste Forel", included in *Bahá'í World Faith*. Wilmette: Bahá'í Publishing Trust, second edn. 1956.

COOPER, L. *An Introduction to the Meaning and Structure of Physics*. New York: Harper & Row, 1968.

FERRIS, TIMOTHY. *Coming of Age in the Milky Way*. New York: Anchor Books, 1989.

GARDNER, MARTIN. *Relativity for the Million*. New York: The Macmillan Company, 1962.

HAWKING, STEPHEN W. *A Brief History of Time*. New York: Bantam Books, 1988.

LEDERMAN, LEON AND TERESI, DICK. *The God Particle*. New York: Dell, 1993.

KOSTRO, LUDWIK. *Einstein and the Ether*. Montreal: C. Roy Keys Inc., 2000.

MISNER, CHARLES W., THORNE, KIP S. AND WHEELER, JOHN A. *Gravitation* San Francisco: Freeman, 1973.

UNIVERSAL HOUSE OF JUSTICE. *Messages from the Universal House of Justice 1968-1986*. Wilmette: Bahá'í Publishing Trust, 1996.

WILBER, KEN, ED. *Quantum Questions: Mystical Writings of the World's Great Physicists*. Boulder & London: Shambhala, 1984.

WILCZEK, FRANK. *The Lightness of Being: Mass, Ether, and the Unification of Forces*. New York: Basic Books, 2010.

WILLIAMS, L. PEARCE. 'Ether', *The Encyclopedia Americana*, 1989, Vol. X, p. 609.

WOLF, FRED ALAN. *Taking the Quantum Leap*. New York: Harper & Rowe, 1981. Perennial Library edn. 1989.

Acknowledgments

Much credit for this book belongs, as always, to my dear wife, Cheri Wallace Matthews. Her unflagging support and encouragement, her patience with my schedule, and her wise feedback on style and substance – all combine to make my writing far better than it otherwise would be. The beautiful cover design is only the most visible of her many contributions.

Among the friends who encouraged me to publish my findings on this book's topic were Kenneth Kalantar, Vahid Alavian, and (far from least) the late Marzieh Gail.

Stephen Friberg and Ian Kluge called my attention to the articles by, respectively, Frank Wilczek and Paul Davies referenced in the text.

Much of the material here is either reprinted or lightly adapted from my earlier book, *The Challenge of Bahá'u'lláh*, first made available in 1993 by George Ronald, Publisher. To that company's wonderful editorial team – May Hofman, Erica Leith, and Wendi Momen – I remain forever indebted.

About the Author

Gary Matthews is a second-generation Bahá'í with a lifelong passion for science and its connections with mystical spirituality. He and his wife, Cheri, are founders of Stonehaven Press in Knoxville, Tennessee, where they live.

Other books by Gary Matthews include *The Challenge of Bahá'u'lláh*, *He Cometh with Clouds*, *Becoming America's Religion*, and *The Metropolis of Satan*.